Color Your Way to Peace

We talk about it all the time: finding peace, enjoying the quiet, spending time alone with the Lord. We quote Psalm 46:10, "Be still, and know that I am God." We talk about heading to a peaceful spot in nature to enjoy the solitude and spend time alone with the Lord.

And then we Instagram the nature around us…

We tweet #Peace and #Blessed about our quiet time…

We pin or post a graphic of our favorite Bible verse…

We remember the long list of tasks that need to be done…

Of course, there's nothing wrong with being busy, nor with technology or social media, but its introduction and inundation in our lives has presented some uniquely modern challenges. Quieting our minds, spending time meditating on the words of the Lord, and entering into a time of quiet reflection and worship is *hard*. We want to spend time with our Lord, we want to be quiet and hear what He has to say, but distractions are literally everywhere. Our minds have been trained to move from topic to topic quickly, and focusing and thinking deeply on one thing can be tough—despite our desires and best efforts.

That's why we've created this book. Within these pages, we hope that you can enter into an immersive time of meditation, reflection, and worship. There is a spiritual practice called *Lectio Divina*—Latin for "divine reading"—where you read Scripture and then meditate and reflect on the words, making yourself open to whatever God wants to reveal to you. While we are in no way suggesting this book replace the time you spend in the Word, we're hoping this can help you train your mind to be still, to focus, to quiet the world around you, and to open yourself up to how God wants to speak to you.

In the pages that follow, you'll find beautiful illustrations surrounding some impactful words from Scripture, hymns, preachers, teachers, and writers. We hope you will read the words and meditate on them as you color. Let the Lord speak to you through the words, through your creativity, and through the action of creating something beautiful.

At the back of this book you'll find a link to a Spotify playlist called "Whatever Is Lovely" to help usher you into a time of worship and reflection. Have it playing in the background as you color and reflect, allowing the words on the page and the song itself to bring you into a sweet time with Christ.

This book is about worship. It's about hearing from our God who only wants to spend time with us, to speak to us, and to grow us. This book is about taking holy meditation, creativity, and art and infusing it into our spiritual practices and quiet times to find a fresh and life-giving way to engage with our Heavenly Father. It's about quieting those distractions that often can be loud and troublesome and finally allowing ourselves to ease into quality time with our Savior. Christ has so much He wants to share with us; we simply need to listen.

Of course, worship is often best shared with others. Why not get a group of friends together and have a coloring night? Gather around a table and share your lives and your stories while sharing your colored pencils.

Finally, if you can't resist the urge to Instagram (who can blame you?), we'd love it if you would Instagram the pages you color with the hashtag #WhateverIsLovely.

Whatever is Lovely

WATERBROOK
PRESS

WHATEVER IS LOVELY
PUBLISHED BY WATERBROOK PRESS
12265 Oracle Boulevard, Suite 200
Colorado Springs, Colorado 80921

Trade Paperback ISBN 978-1-60142-928-5

Published in the United States by WaterBrook Multnomah, an imprint of the Crown Publishing Group, a division of Penguin Random House LLC, New York.

WATERBROOK® and its deer colophon are registered trademarks of Penguin Random House LLC.

Printed in the United States of America
2016

10 9 8 7 6 5 4 3

SPECIAL SALES
Most WaterBrook Multnomah books are available at special quantity discounts when purchased in bulk by corporations, organizations, and special-interest groups. Custom imprinting or excerpting can also be done to fit special needs. For information, please e-mail SpecialMarkets@ WaterBrookMultnomah.com or call 1-800-603-7051.

"Finally, brothers and sisters, whatever is true, whatever is noble, whatever is right, whatever is pure, whatever is lovely, whatever is admirable—if anything is excellent or praiseworthy—think about such things" (Philippians 4:8).

Illustrated and hand-lettered by Holly Camp

FROM THE BEGINNING, GOD CREATED US FOR A DEEP, ABIDING, INTIMATE, EVERLASTING RELATIONSHIP WITH HIM.
— Francine Rivers

From the blog post "Old Testament Lessons," February 7, 2015, at Francine Rivers.com. Francine Rivers is the author of several best-selling novels, including the Christian fiction classic, *Redeeming Love*.

"Again Jesus said, 'Peace be with you! As the Father has sent me, I am sending you'" (John 20:21).

Illustrated by Linda A. Tetmyer
Hand-lettered by Jennifer Tucker

"He has shown you, O mortal, what is good.
     And what does the LORD require of you?
To act justly and to love mercy
     and to walk humbly with your God" (Micah 6:8).

Illustrated by André Cazley
Hand-lettered by Jennifer Tucker

Jesus sought me when a stranger

∴ ROBERT ROBINSON ∴

Come Thou Fount
by Robert Robinson

Come Thou fount of ev'ry blessing,
Tune my heart to sing Thy grace;
Streams of mercy never ceasing
Call for songs of loudest praise.
Teach me some melodious sonnet,
Sung by flaming tongues above.
Praise the mount! I'm fixed upon it,
Mount of Thy redeeming love.

Here I raise my Ebenezer:
Hither by Thy help I've come;
And I hope by Thy good pleasure
Safely to arrive at home.
Jesus sought me when a stranger,
Wand'ring from the fold of God;
He to rescue me from danger
Interposed His precious blood.

O to grace how great a debtor
Daily I'm constrained to be!
Let Thy goodness, like a fetter,
Bind my wand'ring heart to Thee.
Prone to wander, Lord, I feel it,
Prone to leave the God I love;
Here's my heart, Lord, take and seal it,
Seal it for Thy courts above.

"Come Thou Fount" was written in 1757 and is based on 1 Samuel 7:12. The music
for the hymn was composed by Asahel Nettleton in 1813.

Illustrated and hand-lettered by Bridget Hurley

"You, my brothers and sisters, were called to be free. But do not use your freedom to indulge the flesh; rather, serve one another humbly in love" (Galatians 5:13).

Illustrated by Katherine Howe
Hand-lettered by Holly Camp

Corrie ten Boom was a Dutch Christian, who helped many Jews escape the Holocaust during World War II, and was ultimately imprisoned herself. She chronicles her amazing story in *The Hiding Place*.

Illustrated and hand-lettered by Ann-Margret Hovsepian

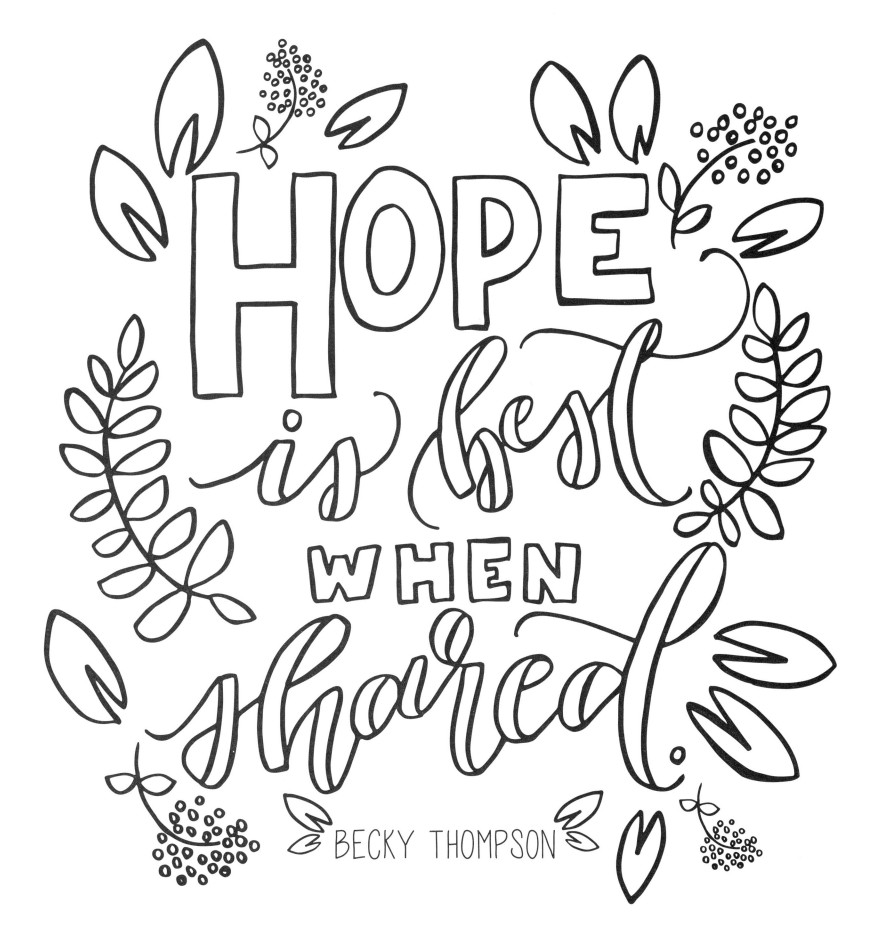

HOPE is best when shared.

— BECKY THOMPSON

Becky Thompson—also known as Scissortail SILK—blogs at BeckyThompson.com and is the author of *Hope Unfolding*.

Illustrated and hand-lettered by Ashley Gardner

"Now then, my children, listen to me;
blessed are those who keep my ways" (Proverbs 8:32).

Illustrated by André Cazley
Hand-lettered by Jennifer Tucker

From the blog post "Peace Amid Chaos: My Word for 2014," January 1, 2014, at NishWeiseth.com. Nish Weiseth is a speaker and the author of the book *Speak*.

Illustrated and hand-lettered by Jennifer Tucker

I am with you always.

MATTHEW 28:20

"Therefore go and make disciples of all nations, baptizing them in the name of the Father and of the Son and of the Holy Spirit, and teaching them to obey everything I have commanded you. And surely I am with you always, to the very end of the age" (Matthew 28:19–20).

Illustrated by Bridget Hurley
Hand-lettered by Holly Camp

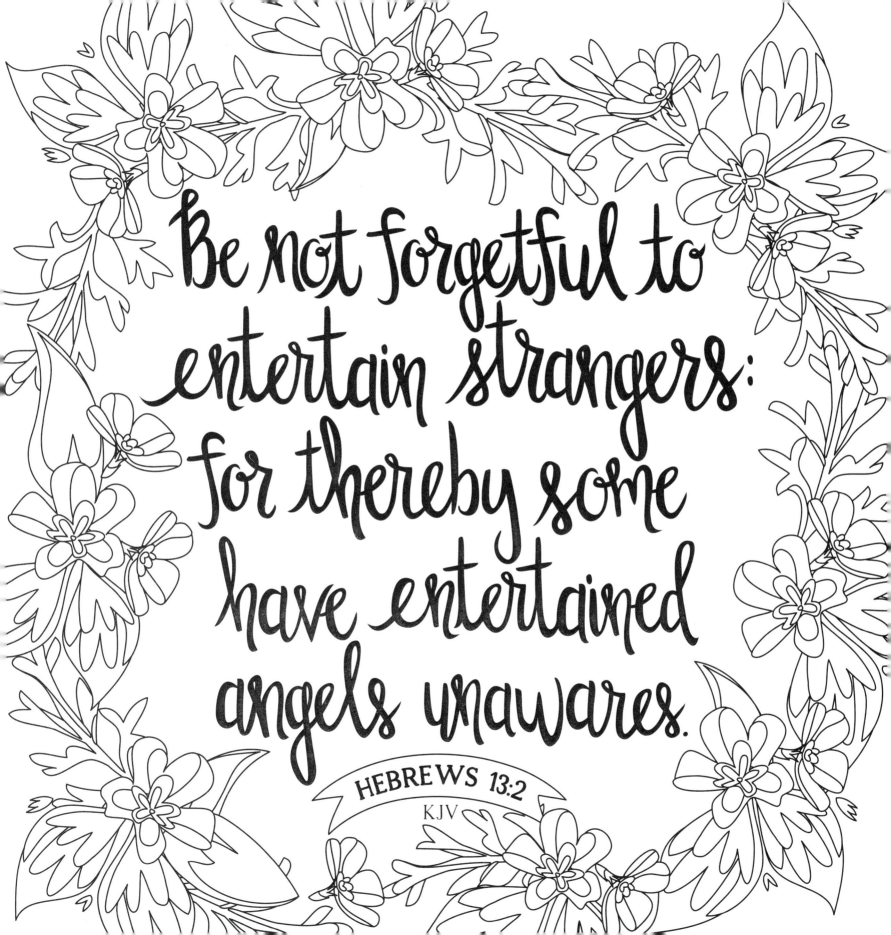

Be not forgetful to entertain strangers: for thereby some have entertained angels unawares.

HEBREWS 13:2
KJV

"Be not forgetful to entertain strangers:
for thereby some have entertained angels
unawares" (Hebrews 13:2, KJV).

Illustrated and hand-lettered by Jenny Stewart

Echoes of mercy
Whispers of love

Frances J. Crosby

Blessed Assurance
by Frances J. Crosby

Blessed assurance; Jesus is mine!
Oh, what a foretaste of glory divine!
Heir of salvation, purchase of God,
Born of His Spirit, washed in His blood.

This is my story, this is my song,
praising my Savior all the day long;
this is my story, this is my song,
praising my Savior all the day long.

Perfect submission, perfect delight!
Visions of rapture now burst on my sight;
Angels descending bring from above
Echoes of mercy, whispers of love.

Perfect submission, all is at rest!
I in my Savior am happy and blest;
Watching and waiting, looking above,
Filled with His goodness, lost in His love.

Crosby, who became blind at the age of six weeks, wrote "Blessed Assurance" after hearing her friend play a new melody on the piano. When asked what the melody sounded like, Crosby replied "Blessed assurance; Jesus is mine." The song is based on an interpretation of Hebrews 10:22: "Let us draw near with a true heart in full assurance of faith, having our hearts sprinkled from an evil conscience, and our bodies washed with pure water" (KJV).

Illustrated by Katherine Howe
Hand-lettered by Holly Camp

Love
NEVER
gives up.

I CORINTHIANS 13 (MSG)

"No matter what I say, what I believe, and what I do, I'm bankrupt without love.
Love never gives up.
Love cares more for others than for self.
Love doesn't want what it doesn't have.
Love doesn't strut,
Doesn't have a swelled head,
Doesn't force itself on others,
Isn't always 'me first,'
Doesn't fly off the handle,
Doesn't keep score of the sins of others,
Doesn't revel when others grovel,
Takes pleasure in the flowering of truth,
Puts up with anything,
Trusts God always,
Always looks for the best,
Never looks back,
But keeps going to the end" (1 Corinthians 13:3–7, MSG).

Illustrated and hand-lettered by Ann-Margret Hovsepian

From the blog post "Love Is Not Weak," May 11, 2011, at RachelHeldEvans.com.
Rachel Held Evans is a speaker and *New York Times* best-selling author.

Illustrated and hand-lettered by Jennifer Tucker

"You yourselves have seen what I did to Egypt, and how I carried you on eagles' wings and brought you to myself" (Exodus 19:4).

Illustrated by Katherine Howe
Hand-lettered by Jennifer Tucker

Do not worry about tomorrow.

Matthew 6:34

"Therefore do not worry about tomorrow, for tomorrow will worry about itself. Each day has enough trouble of its own" (Matthew 6:34).

Illustrated by Linda A. Tetmyer
Hand-lettered by Jennifer Tucker

THE MOON SHINES FULL AT HIS COMMAND, AND ALL THE STARS OBEY.

—ISAAC WATTS

I Sing the Mighty Power of God
by Isaac Watts

I sing the mighty power of God, that made the mountains rise,
That spread the flowing seas abroad, and built the lofty skies.
I sing the wisdom that ordained the sun to rule the day;
The moon shines full at God's command, and all the stars obey.

I sing the goodness of the Lord, who filled the earth with food,
Who formed the creatures through the Word, and then pronounced them good.
Lord, how Thy wonders are displayed, where'er I turn my eye,
If I survey the ground I tread, or gaze upon the sky.

There's not a plant or flower below, but makes Thy glories known,
And clouds arise, and tempests blow, by order from Thy throne;
While all that borrows life from Thee is ever in Thy care;
And everywhere that we can be, Thou, God art present there.

Isaac Watts wrote this hymn for children to sing based on the creation story in Genesis.
Watts, who also wrote "Joy to the World," lived from 1674–1748.

Illustrated by GaiaVerse

it is well
with my soul

HORATIO
G. SPAFFORD

It Is Well with My Soul
by Horatio G. Spafford

When peace, like a river, attendeth my way,
When sorrows like sea billows roll;
Whatever my lot, Thou hast taught me to say,
It is well, it is well, with my soul.

Refrain
It is well, with my soul,
It is well, it is well with my soul.

My sin, oh, the bliss of this glorious thought!
My sin, not in part but the whole,
Is nailed to the cross, and I bear it no more,
Praise the Lord, praise the Lord, O my soul!

And Lord, haste the day when the faith shall be sight,
The clouds be rolled back as a scroll;
The trump shall resound, and the Lord shall descend,
Even so, it is well with my soul.

Horatio G. Spafford, a successful lawyer and real-estate investor in Chicago in the 1870s, suffered a number of tragic losses in a short period of time. Soon after the death of their young son, Horatio and his wife, Anna, lost nearly all of their real-estate investments as a result of the great Chicago fire. As Anna and their four daughters traveled to England to recover from these tragedies, their ship collided with another ship. All four daughters perished. On the journey to join his wife in England, at a spot near that tragic collision, Spafford was inspired by the Holy Spirit to write these words of eternal hope.

Illustrated by Bridget Hurley
Hand-lettered by Jennifer Tucker

"So be truly glad. There is wonderful joy ahead, even though you must endure many trials for a little while. These trials will show that your faith is genuine. It is being tested as fire tests and purifies gold—though your faith is far more precious than mere gold. So when your faith remains strong through many trials, it will bring you much praise and glory and honor on the day when Jesus Christ is revealed to the whole world" (1 Peter 1:6–7, NLT).

Illustrated and hand-lettered by Holly Camp

Let your gentleness be evident.

– Philippians 4:5

"Rejoice in the Lord always. I will say it again: Rejoice! Let your gentleness be evident to all" (Philippians 4:4–5).

Illustrated by Carrie Stephens

A Shelter in the Time of Storm
by Vernon J. Charlesworth

The Lord's our Rock, in Him we hide,
A Shelter in the time of storm;
Secure whatever ill betide,
A Shelter in the time of storm.

Refrain
Oh, Jesus is a Rock in a weary land,
A weary land, a weary land;
Oh, Jesus is a Rock in a weary land,
A Shelter in the time of storm.

A shade by day, defense by night,
A Shelter in the time of storm;
No fears alarm, no foes afright,
A Shelter in the time of storm.

The raging storms may round us beat,
A Shelter in the time of storm;
We'll never leave our safe retreat,
A Shelter in the time of storm.

O Rock divine, O Refuge dear,
A Shelter in the time of storm;
Be Thou our Helper ever near,
A Shelter in the time of storm.

This was a favorite hymn of fishermen in northern England during storms.
Vernon Charlesworth wrote the words around 1880, based on Psalm 32:7.

Illustrated by Katherine Howe
Hand-lettered by Jennifer Tucker

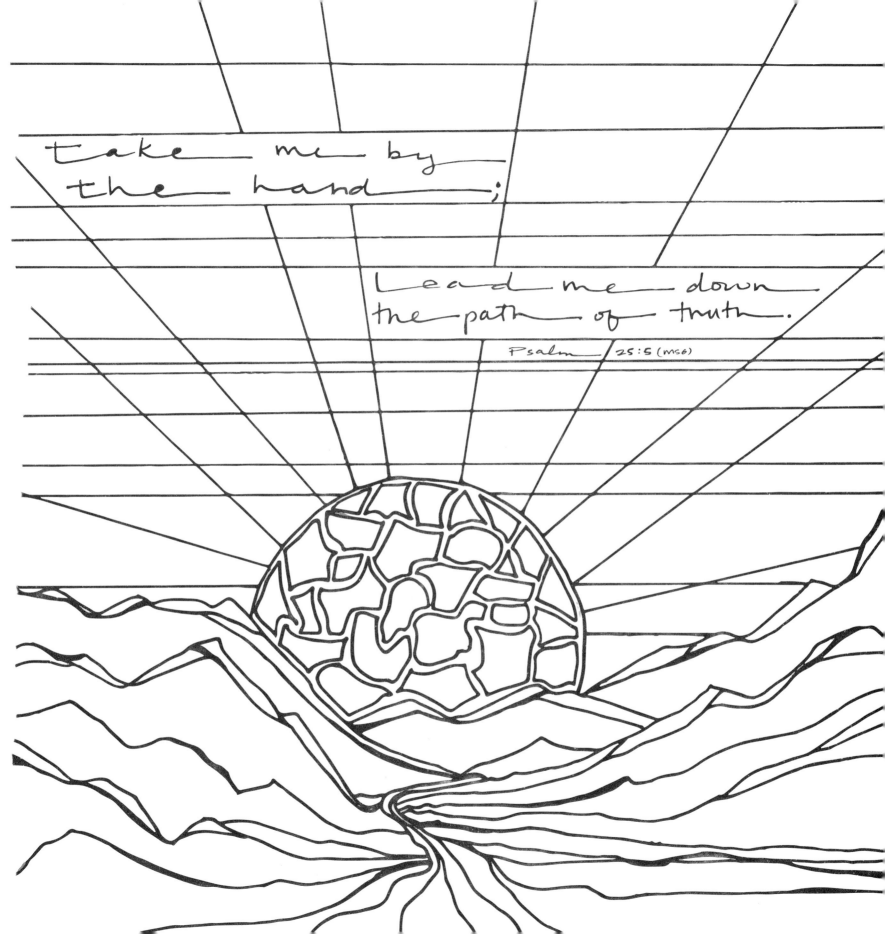

"Show me how you work, GOD;
School me in your ways.

Take me by the hand;
Lead me down the path of truth.
You are my Savior, aren't you?" (Psalm 25:4–5, MSG).

Illustrated and hand-lettered by Lisa Shirk

From the blog post "Make Your First 5 Count," May 8, 2015, at LysaTerkeurst.com.
Lysa is a *New York Times* best-selling author and president of Proverbs 31 Ministries.

Illustrated and hand-lettered by Ann-Margret Hovsepian

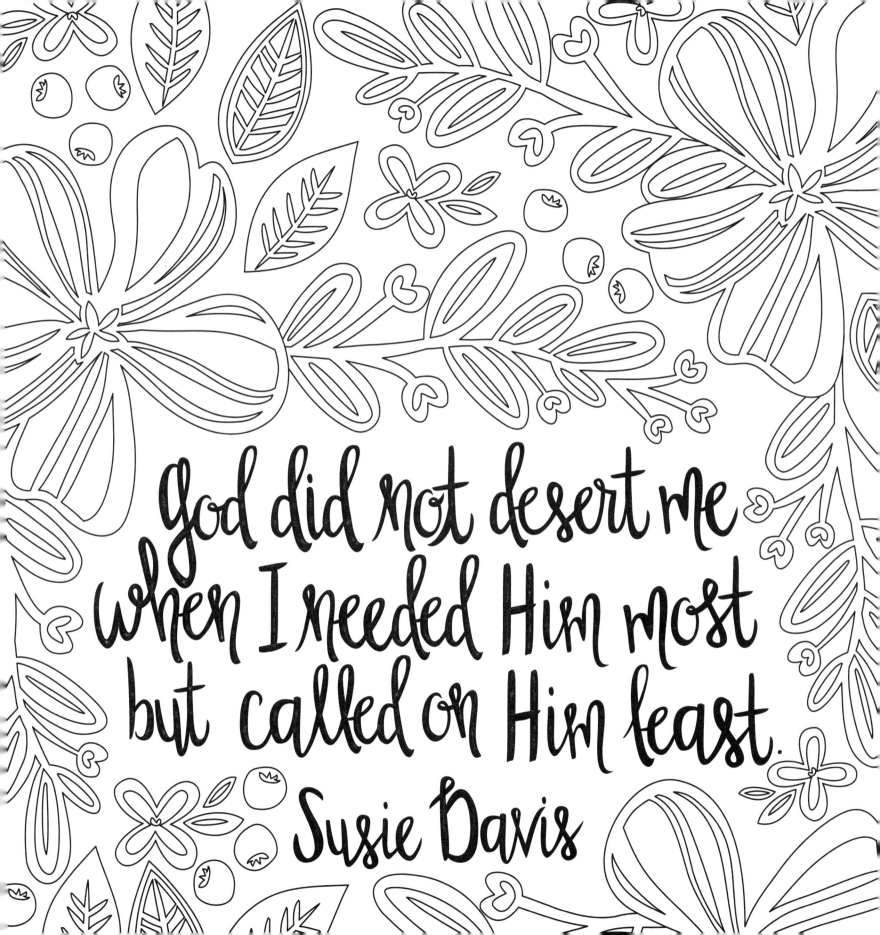

God did not desert me when I needed Him most but called on Him least.

Susie Davis

From the blog post "Becoming: The Good News Girl" at SusieDavis.org.
Susie Davis is the author of the book *Unafraid*.

Illustrated and hand-lettered by Jenny Stewart

GOD HAS PROMISED
STRENGTH FOR THE DAY.

-ANNIE J. FLINT

What God Hath Promised
by Annie Johnson Flint

God has not promised skies always blue,
Flower-strewn pathways all our lives through;
God has not promised sun without rain,
Joy without sorrow, peace without pain.

Refrain
But God has promised strength for the day,
Rest for the labor, light for the way,
Grace for the trials, help from above,
Unfailing kindness, undying love.

God has not promised we shall not know
Toil and temptation, trouble and woe;
He has not told us we shall not bear
Many a burden, many a care.

God has not promised smooth roads and wide,
Swift, easy travel, needing no guide;
Never a mountain rocky and steep,
Never a river turbid and deep.

This was the last hymn written by Annie Johnson Flint. She was orphaned as a young child and lost her adoptive parents several years later. Flint struggled with severe arthritis that left her bedridden in her late twenties. She typed this hymn with her knuckles as she barely had the use of her hands. She passed away at the age of sixty-three.

Illustrated by GaiaVerse

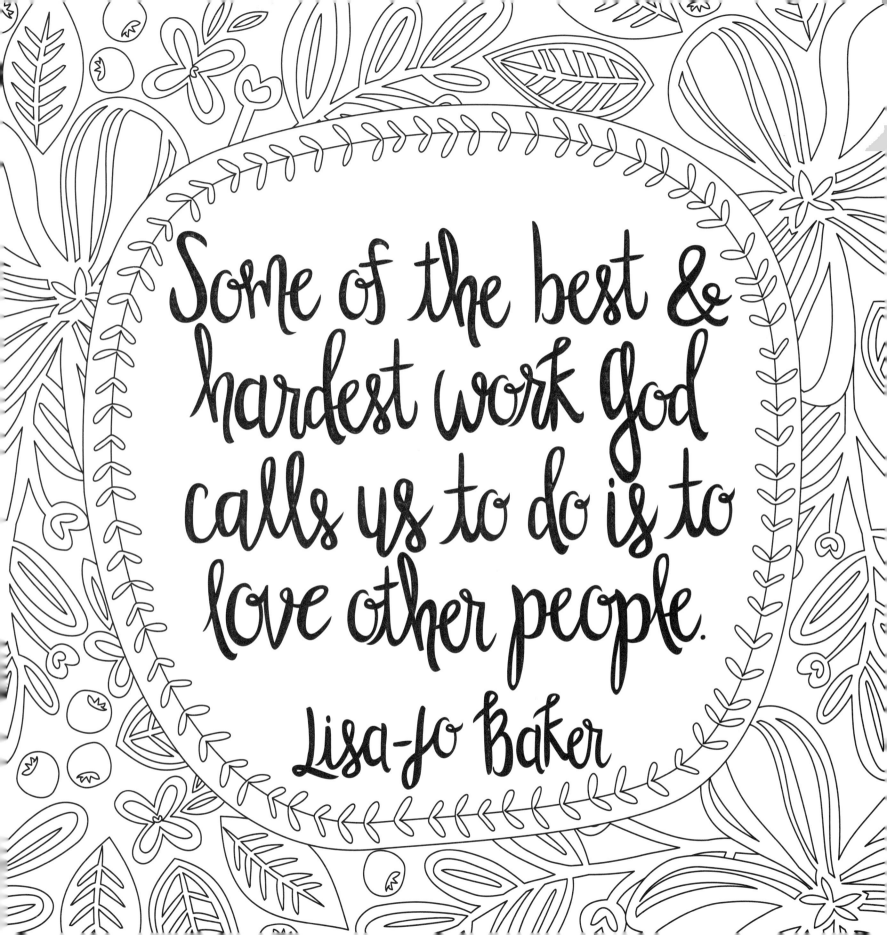

From the blog post "6 Helpful Ways to Respond to Hard Conversations," July 23, 2015, at incourage.me. Lisa-Jo Baker is the author of the book *Surprised by Motherhood* and is the community manager for (in)courage.

Illustrated and hand-lettered by Jenny Stewart

'Tis so Sweet to Trust in Jesus
by Louisa M.R. Stead

'Tis so sweet to trust in Jesus,
Just to take Him at His Word;
Just to rest upon His promise,
And to know, "Thus saith the Lord!"

Refrain
Jesus, Jesus, how I trust Him!
How I've proved Him o'er and o'er;
Jesus, Jesus, precious Jesus!
Oh, for grace to trust Him more!

Oh, how sweet to trust in Jesus,
Just to trust His cleansing blood;
And in simple faith to plunge me
'Neath the healing, cleansing flood!

Yes, 'tis sweet to trust in Jesus,
Just from sin and self to cease;
Just from Jesus simply taking
Life and rest, and joy and peace.

I'm so glad I learned to trust Thee,
Precious Jesus, Savior, Friend;
And I know that Thou art with me,
Wilt be with me to the end.

Louisa Stead and her husband and young daughter were enjoying a picnic on Long Island when they were interrupted by a boy screaming. Her husband rushed into the water to save a drowning boy, but they both drowned, as Louisa and her daughter watched in horror. "'Tis so Sweet to Trust in Jesus" was written in 1882, in the period of hardship following the death of her husband.

Illustrated and hand-lettered by Lisa Shirk

there is not ONE SINGLE atom or iota or dash or wisp THAT IS BEYOND God's ability to REDEEM

Deidra Riggs

From the blog post "Everything New," February 28, 2015, on incourage.me. Deidra Riggs is the author of *Every Little Thing: Making a World of Difference Right Where You Are* (Baker Books, 2015) and blogs at DeidraRiggs.com.

Illustrated and hand-lettered by Jennifer Tucker

Be still
and
know that
I am God.
Psalm 46:10

"Come and see what the LORD has done,
    the desolations he has brought on the earth.
He makes wars cease
    to the ends of the earth.
He breaks the bow and shatters the spear;
    he burns the shields with fire.
He says, 'Be still, and know that I am God;
    I will be exalted among the nations,
    I will be exalted in the earth.'

The LORD Almighty is with us;
    the God of Jacob is our fortress" (Psalm 46:8–11).

Illustrated by Bridget Hurley
Hand-lettered by Jennifer Tucker

my grace is sufficient for you.

2 CORINTHIANS 12:9

"But he said to me, 'My grace is sufficient for you, for my power is made perfect in weakness.' Therefore I will boast all the more gladly about my weaknesses, so that Christ's power may rest on me. That is why, for Christ's sake, I delight in weaknesses, in insults, in hardships, in persecutions, in difficulties. For when I am weak, then I am strong" (2 Corinthians 12:9–10).

Illustrated by Linda A. Tetmyer
Hand-lettered by Jennifer Tucker

From the blog post "#TellHisStory: Your Sacred Yes," June 16, 2015, at JenniferDukesLee.com. Jennifer Dukes Lee is the author of the book *Love Idol*.

Illustrated and hand-lettered by Ashley Gardner

HOW YOU FEEL
DOES NOT CHANGE
THE TRUTH OF THIS:
YOU ARE LOVED,
LOVED, LOVED.

—SARAH BESSEY

From the blog post "To the Young Women Reading 'Jesus Feminist,'" July 20, 2015, at SarahBessey.com. Sarah is an author and speaker.

Illustrated by Carrie Stephens

Softly and Tenderly
by Will L. Thompson

Softly and tenderly Jesus is calling,
Calling for you and for me;
See, on the portals He's waiting and watching,
Watching for you and for me.

Refrain:
Come home, come home,
You who are weary, come home;
Earnestly, tenderly, Jesus is calling,
Calling, O sinner, come home!

Why should we tarry when Jesus is pleading,
Pleading for you and for me?
Why should we linger and heed not His mercies,
Mercies for you and for me?

Time is now fleeting, the moments are passing,
Passing from you and from me;
Shadows are gathering, deathbeds are coming,
Coming for you and for me.

Oh, for the wonderful love He has promised,
Promised for you and for me!
Though we have sinned, He has mercy and pardon,
Pardon for you and for me.

Will Thompson made the decision to write Christian music and hymns after attending an evangelistic meeting held by Dwight L. Moody. Thompson wrote "Softly and Tenderly" in 1880, and Moody used it as an invitation hymn in his meetings. On Moody's deathbed, he told Thompson that he would have rather written "Softly and Tenderly" than anything he had been able to do in his own life.

Illustrated and hand-lettered by Ann-Margret Hovsepian

I Need Thee Every Hour
by Annie S. Hawks

I need Thee every hour, most gracious Lord;
No tender voice like Thine can peace afford.

Refrain
I need Thee, oh, I need Thee;
Every hour I need Thee;
Oh, bless me now, my Savior,
I come to Thee.

I need Thee every hour, stay Thou nearby;
Temptations lose their pow'r when Thou art nigh.

I need Thee every hour, in joy or pain;
Come quickly and abide, or life is vain.

I need Thee every hour; teach me Thy will;
And Thy rich promises in me fulfill.

I need Thee every hour, most Holy One;
Oh, make me Thine indeed, Thou blessed Son.

Annie S. Hawks wrote over four hundred hymns in her eighty-three years, but "I Need Thee Every Hour" remains the most beloved. Hawks wrote the lyrics one day in the midst of her everyday duties. She felt an overwhelming nearness to God and wondered how anyone could live without that presence in joy or in pain. Her pastor, Robert S. Lowery, wrote the music, and the hymn was published immediately. Hawks didn't fully realize the comfort her words written from joyfulness had provided to those in pain until she lost her husband several years later.

Illustrated and hand-lettered by Lisa Shirk

"You will be secure, because there is hope;
        you will look about you and take your rest in safety" (Job 11:18).

Illustrated and hand-lettered by Ann-Margret Hovsepian

All Creatures of Our God and King

by St. Francis of Assisi (paraphrased by William Draper)

All creatures of our God and King
Lift up your voice and with us sing:
Alleluia! Alleluia!
Thou burning sun with golden beam,
Thou silver moon with softer gleam!

Refrain
O praise Him! O praise Him!
Alleluia! Alleluia!

Thou rushing wind that art so strong,
Ye clouds that sail in heaven along,
O praise Him! Alleluia!
Thou rising moon, in praise rejoice,
Ye lights of evening, find a voice!

Let all things their Creator bless,
And worship Him in humbleness,
O praise Him! Alleluia!
Praise, praise the Father, praise the Son,
And praise the Spirit, Three in One!

Francis of Assisi wrote the words to this hymn around 1225, but it wasn't published until the early 1600s. It was translated to English and paraphrased by William Draper in the early 1900s. Francis is known as the patron saint of animals and the environment.

Illustrated and hand-lettered by Holly Camp

Let the words of my mouth, and the meditation of my heart, be acceptable in thy sight, O Lord.

Psalm 19:14 (KJV)

"Let the words of my mouth, and the meditation of my heart, be acceptable in thy sight, O LORD, my strength, and my redeemer" (Psalm 19:14, KJV).

Illustrated and hand-lettered by Lisa Shirk

Doxology

by Thomas Ken

Praise God, from Whom all blessings flow;
Praise Him all creatures here below;
Praise Him above, ye heav'nly host;
Praise Father, Son, and Holy Ghost.
Amen

These words, written in 1674, are the last verse of a longer hymn, "Awake, My Soul, and with the Sun." A doxology is a short hymn of praise to God.

Illustrated and hand-lettered by Holly Camp

Based on Psalm 147:4, from the blog "The One Who Names the Stars," July 16, 2015, at LizCurtisHiggs.com. Liz Curtis Higgs is a speaker and the best-selling author of *The Women of Christmas* and many other books.

Illustrated by Katherine Howe
Hand-lettered by Jennifer Tucker

"He has made everything beautiful in its time. He has also set eternity in the human heart; yet no one can fathom what God has done from beginning to end" (Ecclesiastes 3:11).

Illustrated and hand-lettered by Jennifer Tucker

Artists, Illustrators, and Hand-Letterers

We'd like to give a big thank you to the following dozen people for sharing their creativity on the pages of this book. We handed them the text and set them loose to illustrate it in their own unique styles. You can check out their websites and Etsy sites to see more of their art and learn more about them.

Holly Camp (HollyCampCards.etsy.com)
André Cazley (Etsy.com/shop/cazdesignshop)
GaiaVerse (Etsy.com/shop/GaiaVerse)
Ashley Gardner (PrintableWisdomCo.com)
Ann-Margret Hovsepian (AnnHovsepian.com)
Katherine Howe (GracefullyPenned.wordpress.com)
Bridget Hurley (BlueSkyBeads.Etsy.com)
Lisa Shirk (LisaShirk.com)
Carrie Stephens (FishScraps.Etsy.com)
Jenny Stewart (FrenchPressMornings.com)
Linda A. Tetmyer (SnowflakeEclecticArt.etsy.com)
Jennifer Tucker (LittleHouseStudio.net)

WaterBrook Press

Thank you to all of the individuals and departments within WaterBrook Press for their help in creating this book—in particular Lori Addicott, Laura Barker, Candice Chaplin, Tina Constable, Alex Field, Bridget Givan, Ginia Hairston Croker, Debbie Mitchell, Kristopher Orr, Beverly Rykerd, Sara Selkirk, Pam Shoup, and Julia Wallace. We'd especially like to thank Karen Sherry for her talent, time, and fortitude in the design and typesetting process.

Whatever Is Lovely Development Team

Kendall Davis
Jessica Gingrich
Amy Haddock
Jessica Lamb
Susan Tjaden

Playlist

We truly want this book to help you engage in a rich worship experience and to be uplifting to your soul and spirit. Music speaks so much deeper than just words, so we've created a playlist of songs to listen to while you create your unique work of art. We know the result will be beautiful.

https://open.spotify.com/user/waterbrookmultnomah
Playlist: Whatever Is Lovely